DISCOVER
Water

BY NADIA HIGGINS • ILLUSTRATED BY JANE YAMADA

PUBLISHED by The Child's World®
1980 Lookout Drive • Mankato, MN 56003-1705
800-599-READ • www.childsworld.com

ACKNOWLEDGMENTS

The Child's World®: Mary Berendes, Publishing Director
The Design Lab: Design
Jody Jensen Shaffer: Editing
Pamela J. Mitsakos: Photo Research

PHOTO CREDITS

© altanaka/Shutterstock.com: 5; Andrey Starostin/Shutterstock.com: 7; Ariena/
Shutterstock.com: 10; Denis Tabler/Shutterstock.com: 8; DrRave/iStock.com: 18; Egon
NYC/Shutterstock.com: 12; Kichigin/Shutterstock.com: 9; Jag_cz/Shutterstock.com:
cover, 1; Mike Flippo/Shutterstock.com: 15; Montypeter/Shutterstock.com: 17; Nadja
Rider/Shutterstock.com: 11; orxy/Shutterstock.com: 6; punnaphob/Shutterstock.com:
19; tammykayphoto/Shutterstock.com: 13; yanikap/Shutterstock.com: 16

ISBN 9781626873070
LCCN 2014930659

PRINTED in the United States of America • Mankato, MN
July, 2014 • PA02220

CONTENTS

WET WATER

Drink it.

Spill it.

Splash it.

Spray it.

Water is wet.

It is a **liquid**.

It is fun to splash in water on a hot summer day.

Liquid water rains down from clouds. It rushes in rivers and fills lakes.

Water can be found deep underground.

Water is also found above ground.

It soaks deep into the ground. It swirls in the ocean and crashes on the shore.

COLD, HARD ICE

But liquid water changes. It gets cold. It freezes. It becomes hard ice.

Ice can be smooth or bumpy.

Ice chunks float on a lake.

A snowflake is made of ice. It is full of holes, like lace. When snowflakes pile up, they make white, fluffy snow.

A snowflake usually has six sides.

Snow blankets the ground on a calm winter day.

The coldest parts of Earth are covered in sheets of ice. **Glaciers** creep over land. Giant ice chunks float on the Arctic Ocean.

A glacier is a slow-moving river of ice.

The warm sun melts an icicle.

But ice changes. It warms up. It melts back into liquid water.

13

INVISIBLE WATER VAPOR

If water warms up enough, it changes another way. It breaks up into bits too tiny to see. They float away. They become **water vapor.** Water vapor is part of invisible air.

Clothes dry because water has turned into water vapor.

Fog is like a cloud that is close to the ground.

But then water vapor changes. It cools down.
It forms tiny drops of liquid water.

The drops may form clouds in the sky, or **fog** over land, or **dew** that coats the grass in the morning.

Dew sparkles in the sunlight.

AMAZING WATER

Most of Earth is covered by water. And it's a good thing, too.

The blue areas are Earth's oceans.

A tree's roots seek water deep under the ground.

Plants suck up water with their thirsty roots. People and animals slurp it up, too. Every living thing needs water to stay alive.

Think of all the ways you use water:

for drinking

for cooking

for washing

for flushing.

And water never runs out! It just keeps changing among its three forms.

THE THREE FORMS OF WATER

Water vapor is a gas. It is part of invisible air.

Water is a liquid. It is wet.

Ice is a solid. It is cold and hard.

GLOSSARY

dew (DOO): Dew is tiny drops of water. Dew covers grass, cars, and other outdoor things on cool mornings.

fog (FOG): Fog is like a cloud that is near to the ground. Fog is a mass of tiny water droplets.

glaciers (GLAY-shurz): Glaciers are huge, frozen rivers of ice. Glaciers creep along land on Earth's coldest places.

liquid (LIH-kwid): A liquid is something wet that you can pour. Water is a liquid.

water vapor (WAH-tur VAY-pur): Water vapor is made of tiny, floating bits of water. Water vapor is part of invisible air.

TO LEARN MORE

In the Library

Lyon, George Ella. *All the Water in the World.* New York: Atheneum Books for Young Readers, 2011.

Rauzon, Mark J., and Cynthia Overbeck Bix. *Water, Water Everywhere.* San Francisco: Sierra Club Books for Children, 1994.

Wick, Walter. *A Drop Of Water: A Book of Science and Wonder.* New York: Scholastic, 1997.

On the Web

Visit our Web site for lots of links about Water:

www.childsworld.com/links

Note to Parents, Teachers, and Librarians: We routinely check our Web links to make sure they're safe, active sites—so encourage your readers to check them out!

INDEX